MARTIAL ARTS

KARATE

Raintree www.raintreepublishers.co.uk

To order:
Phone 44 (0) 1865 888112
Send a fax to 44 (0) 1865 314091
Visit the Raintree bookshop at
www.raintreepublishers.co.uk
to browse our catalogue and order online.

Produced by
David West **Children's Books**
7 Princeton Court
55 Felsham Road
London SW15 1AZ

Photographer: Sylvio Dokov
Designer: Gary Jeffrey
Editor: Gail Bushnell

First published in Great Britain by
Raintree, Halley Court, Jordan Hill,
Oxford OX2 8EJ, part of Harcourt Education.
Raintree is a registered trademark of Harcourt
Education Ltd.

Printed and bound in Italy

ISBN 1 844 21692 6 (hardback)
07 06 05 04 03
10 9 8 7 6 5 4 3 2 1

ISBN 1 844 21697 7 (paperback))
08 07 06 05 04
10 9 8 7 6 5 4 3 2 1

British Library Cataloguing in Publication Data
Cook, Harry
Karate. – (Martial Arts)
796.8'153
A full catalogue record for this book is available

Acknowledgements
The publishers would like to thank the following for
permission to reproduce photographs:

Abbreviations: t-top, m-middle, b-bottom, r-right,
l-left, c-centre.

Cover & pages - 11t, 12t, 13t, 16t, 20l, 27mr (Jed
Jacobsohn), 26bl (Matthew Stockman), 6tr & br -
Getty Images.

Every effort has been made to contact copyright
holders of any material reproduced in this book.
Any omissions will be rectified in subsequent
printings.if notice is given to the publishers.

Sylvio Dokov was born in Sofia, Bulgaria. For the
past two decades, he has been one of Europe's
leading martial arts photographers. Sylvio works
from his own studio in Telford, Shropshire.

THE AUTHOR
Harry Cook (4th dan) is the chief instructor of the
Seijnhai Karate-Do Association.
THE MODELS
Left – Katy Cook (1st dan)
Right – Josh Learman (1st dan)

An explanation of Japanese karate terms can be

MARTIAL ARTS

KARATE

Harry Cook

Raintree

Contents

Introduction

Karate-do, the 'way of the empty hand' is usually taught as a means of physical and mental training, a method of self-defence and a modern, international competitive sport. Training in karate-do is said to be like taking a long journey on foot. Sometimes the path is easy and sometimes very steep, but the views are always interesting. On your karate journey you can experience all the different aspects of training, but the first step is to gain some understanding of the basic techniques.

History

The history of karate begins in China, where the most famous centre of martial arts was the Shaolin Temple in Honan Province. Chinese martial arts spread to the island of Okinawa where they blended with Okinawan methods to produce karate, a name which originally meant 'China hand'. In 1609, Okinawa was invaded by Japanese samurai from Satsuma who were equipped with guns. The Okinawans had never seen guns and were shocked by the effect of the weapons. One Okinawan warrior wrote 'fire from the end of a staff burnt my nose!'. At the end of the 19th century, the traditional secrecy surrounding karate techniques began to disappear, and in 1922, an Okinawan teacher, Gichin Funakoshi, opened a karate *dojo* (training hall) in Tokyo, Japan. In the 1930s, the characters used to write China hand were changed to mean 'empty hand', although the sound (karate) remained the same.

The Japanese Samurai who invaded Okinawa outlawed the practice of traditional hand-to-hand combat.

Gichin Funakoshi

Demonstrations of karate during the 1950s helped to popularize the sport across the world.

Clothing & etiquette

Before the development of the modern karate training suit, karate students on Okinawa wore a *fundoshi*, or loincloth. When karate was taken to Japan in 1922, a lighter version of the training suit used in judo was developed for karate training.

The karate suit is made up of a jacket and a pair of trousers, usually made of strong white cotton cloth fastened by cloth tapes at the waist and hips.

BELTS

The colour of the belt indicates the grade of the student. Higher grades are awarded on the basis of technique, sparring and understanding of karate.

ungraded
9th *kyu*
8th *kyu*
7th *kyu*
6th *kyu*
5th *kyu*
4th *kyu*
3rd *kyu*
2nd *kyu*
1st *kyu*
dan grades

1

2

3

4

HOW TO TIE THE BELT

1 Place the centre of the belt across your stomach.
2 Cross the belt over your back and bring the belt around to the front.
3 Cross the right end of the belt over the left, and under both layers of cloth.
4 Tie a square knot.

A karate class usually starts with a series of warm-up exercises. The upper body, waist, back and legs are stretched. Strength and stamina are built by performing push-ups, sit-ups and squats.

Bowing is used to show respect. You bow at the beginning and end of a class, and to a partner when training.

Karate basics

Training in karate is usually divided into three parts; kihon (basics), kata (form), and kumite (sparring). These three parts work together to develop effective techniques for both self defence and competition. Power, stamina and flexibility are developed both by training in techniques and by use of special training exercises.

Stances (*tachi*) are the foundations of karate, used to carry the attack to your opponent, move away from an attack, protect the body from attack and provide a solid base for punching, kicking and blocking.

FRONT STANCE
(*zenkutsu dachi*)

Bend the knee of the front leg until the shin is vertical. Straighten the back leg with the knee and ankle joint held firmly, as if the edge of the foot was pushing into the ground. Point the toes of the rear foot forwards, and keep the back straight.

Move the rear leg forwards in a slight curve as if protecting the groin. Do not bend forwards or sideways, and keep the shoulders relaxed. Keep the knees slightly bent. Push the body forwards into the next front stance.

BACK STANCE
(kokutsu dachi)

The movement of weight backwards can be used to unbalance an opponent who might have grabbed your lapels or throat.

1 Both knees are bent and the centre of gravity of the body is held over the rear foot. Place the heel of the front foot at a right angle to the rear foot. The edge of the rear foot should push into the ground.

2 Move the back foot forwards until the knees are together.

3 Step forwards into the back stance. Keep the back straight and the shoulders relaxed.

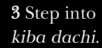

STRADDLE STANCE
(kiba dachi)

Kiba dachi is used defensively by standing sideways to the opponent, or as the ready position when practising side kicks.

1 Put the feet about two shoulder widths apart in a parallel position, and push the outer edges of the feet into the floor. Allow the knees to bend, creating a bow shape with the legs.

2 Move the rear foot across the front foot. Do not lean forwards.

3 Step into *kiba dachi.*

Standing punch
(choku zuki)

This is the most basic way to train the karate punch. The returning hand should feel as if you have grabbed and pulled an opponent into the punch.

To make a correct fist, open both of your hands flat. Fold back the fingers at the first knuckles, then roll up the fingers into a tight fist. Bind the fingers tightly with the thumb. When striking a target, hit with the first two knuckles only.

1

2

3

1 Stand in a natural stance with the feet shoulder-width apart. Push one hand to the front and place the other at the ready position on the hip (palm up). **2** Move the punching hand to the front, while pulling the extended arm back level. **3** Complete the punch. Pull down strongly with the muscles on the shoulders, and use the twisting power generated by the hips.

nge punch
uki)

he basic stepping punch
n most styles of karate.
l to practise this
e in *zenkutsu dachi*,
nce, but other basic
an also be used.

Driving directly forwards with a strong basic punch to score a point.

ont stance and
ont hand, fist
hed.

Move the back foot forwards
until the knees and ankles
are together.

Step forwards and punch.

Reverse punch
(gyaku zuki)

Gyaku zuki, or reverse punch, is performed like *oi zuki* but with the opposite side of the body – if the right leg is forward then the punch is performed with the left fist, and vice versa.

Use a fast hip rotation to drive the punch to the target.

Stand in a front stance and extend the arm which is opposite your front leg.

Move the back foot forwards until the knees and ankles are together.

Continue to step forwards with the same leg and perform a reverse punch.

Jab punch
(kizami zuki)

Kizami zuki resembles a boxing jab. When training, you must use good control to avoid damaging your partner's face.

Both of these contestants are neutralizing each other's attacks, by blocking and using correct distance. The first one to follow up will win.

1

2

1 Stand in a fighting stance.
2 Push forwards with the front foot while simultaneously punching with the front fist. Do not pull the punching hand backwards while pushing the body forwards. Concentrate on driving strongly forwards, to add power to the technique and to achieve the correct distance.

Rising block
(age uke)

1

Blocking in traditional karate is very important. Gichin Funakoshi taught that 'there is no first attack in karate' and so a good defence is necessary.

It is possible to deflect powerful kicks with the forearm using age uke.

Outside block
(soto uke)

1

In basic training, it is usual to use this block against a punch, but in more advanced training, *soto uke* can be used to break a grip, such as a grab to the lapels or a strangle.

If an opponent grabs your lapels use a soto uke to break the grip. Care is needed not to land a full power block on the elbow joint in training, as the arm can be badly damaged.

2

3

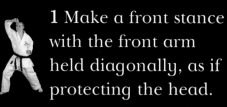

1 Make a front stance with the front arm held diagonally, as if protecting the head.

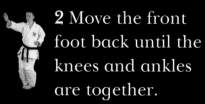

2 Move the front foot back until the knees and ankles are together.

3 Step back with the same leg and perform a rising block by driving the arm up and across the face. The power of the block is increased if a strong twisting action of the hips is used with the movement.

2

3

1 Make a front stance with the front arm held in front of the chest.

2 Move the front foot back level and extend the front arm.

3 Bring the forearm in a curve across the chest as if deflecting an incoming punch. Use a strong twisting action of the hips and forearm and keep a strong stance.

Inside block
(uchi uke)

Uchi uke is performed by moving the forearm in an outward curve from the hip or waist, and is generally used to defend the chest and stomach area.

Blocking a roundhouse kick to the body with gedan barai.

1 Stand in a front stance with the front arm held palm upwards and elbow bent. **2 Move the front foot back** until the knees and ankles are together. Straighten the lead hand (right) and place the other hand, palm down, across the chest. **3 Step back** into a front stance, rotate the forearm (left) up and out as if deflecting a punch.

In close combat *uchi uke* may be used to break an attacker's hold on the wrist while simultaneously upsetting his balance and body posture.

Down block
(gedan barai)

Gedan barai is performed by moving the forearm downwards, as if intercepting a blow aimed at the stomach. In general, this block should be used with a slight side-step to avoid taking the full power of the kick on the arm.

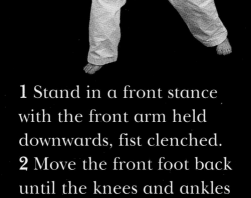

1 Stand in a front stance with the front arm held downwards, fist clenched. **2** Move the front foot back until the knees and ankles are together. Place the fist of the rear hand on the opposite shoulder. **3** Step back into a front stance, move the blocking hand down in a smooth curve as if deflecting a punch or kick.

Knifehand block
(shuto uke)

Knifehand block is often the first open hand block taught to beginners and is usually practised in back stance. The movement of the body weight over the rear leg can be used to unbalance an attacker who may have grabbed the wrist or clothing of the defender.

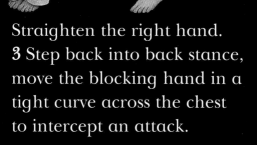

1 Stand in a back stance with the left hand across the chest. **2** Move the front foot back and the blocking hand to the opposite shoulder. Straighten the right hand. **3** Step back into back stance, move the blocking hand in a tight curve across the chest to intercept an attack.

Back fist
(*uraken*)

Uraken is performed by snapping the fist towards a target in a curved motion, using the elbow like a hinge, with the hips adding extra speed.

1

1 Point the elbow at the target with the closed fist touching the chest, palm down. **2** Move the fist in a curve, striking the target with the knuckles. Some instructors say that the wrist should curve in slightly, just before the hand hits the target. **3** Snap the fist back to the ready position. Do not damage the arm by jerking the elbow joint.

2

3

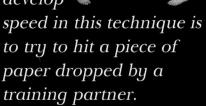

One good way to develop speed in this technique is to try to hit a piece of paper dropped by a training partner.

Elbow
(*empi* or *hiji*)

The elbow is used when close to an opponent. Hit with the point of the elbow, and use the hips to add speed.

The elbow can be used to the side (*yoko empi*). Rising elbow strikes (*age empi*) are used to attack an opponent's jaw. Rear strikes (*ushiro empi*) are used when grabbed from behind.

yoko empi

ushiro empi

age empi

Front kick
(mae geri)

The most direct kick used in karate – *mae geri* – is a very powerful technique, mainly used to strike the stomach or groin.

1 Stand in a fighting stance.

2 Lift the knee of the kicking leg as high as possible.

3 Drive the lower part of the leg forwards. Curl back the toes so the ball of the foot hits the target.

4 Snap the kick back quickly to prevent it being caught. It is important to keep the knee of the supporting leg slightly bent with the foot flat. Push the hips and stomach forwards as the kick hits.

1   2   3   4

Improve the front kick by kicking over a karate belt which is resting on a couple of chairs. If the knee is too low the toes will clip the belt. Keep the knee high to stop the leg swinging upwards instead of driving directly to the target.

Side kick
(yoko geri)

This kick uses the edge of the foot *(sokuto)* to strike the target. The side kick is a very powerful movement. Two basic forms of side kick are used – the side thrust kick (*yoko geri kekomi*), and the side snap kick (*yoko geri keage*).

1   2

An article published in Scientific American *(April 1979) says that 'in a well placed side kick the foot can withstand roughly 2000 times more force than concrete can'. The force of a well executed side kick is immense.*

SIDE THRUST KICK
(yoko geri kekomi)

1 Stand in a straddle stance (*kiba dachi*).

2 Move the rear foot forwards and step over the front of the supporting leg.

3 Lift the knee of the kicking leg as high as possible with the edge of the foot parallel to the floor.

4 Drive the foot in a straight line to the target. Twist the hips and the supporting leg to add power to the kick.

5 Pull the kicking foot back close to the supporting leg.

6 Step forwards into *kiba dachi*.

3 **4** **5** **6**

1 **2** **3** **4** **5**

SIDE SNAP KICK *(yoko geri keage)*
1 Stand in a straddle stance (*kiba dachi*).
2 Move the rear foot forwards and step over the front of the supporting leg.
3 Lift the knee of the kicking leg as high as possible with the edge of the foot parallel to the floor.
4 Snap the foot in a rising curve to the target.
5 Pull the kicking foot back close to the supporting leg, and step forwards into *kiba dachi*.

Using a chair to balance and practise the side thrust kick, imagine the kick is penetrating a target, not simply touching the surface.

Back kick
(ushiro geri)

A powerful technique which involves strong leg and hip muscles, the back kick is used when attacked from behind.

Use a target such as a rolled up newspaper or a focus pad to develop accuracy.

1 Stand in a fighting stance.

2 Twist the body around into a cat stance, turning the head to look at the target.

3 Lift the knee of the kicking leg and thrust the kick to full extension in a straight line. Keep the toes pointing to the ground and strike the target with the heel.

4 Pull the leg back and keep looking at the target.

1

Roundhouse kick
(mawashi geri)

Mawashi geri can be thought of as a hook punch performed with the leg. The knee is lifted high and then moved in a curve to the target.

Use a partner to help you improve your balance and extension of the kick.

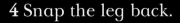

1 Stand in a fighting stance.

2 Lift the kicking leg and point the knee at the target.

3 Snap the leg to full extension. Strike with the instep, being sure to twist the hips and supporting ankle.

4 Snap the leg back.

1

2   3   4

2   3   4

Form
(kata)

Kata, often called 'the heart of karate' are fixed sequences of blocks, punches, kicks, strikes, throws and locks performed in a pattern – called form. They develop good technique and improve physical conditioning.

World kata *champion Tsuguo Sakumoto*

1

5

10

KIHON KATA

Kihon kata was developed in the late 1930s. These photographs only show half of the *kata*. The second half is a repetition of the techniques shown here; so number 13 duplicates number 2. After the last punch (same as number 11), repeat movements 2–6.

1 *Yoi* (ready). Take natural stance and grip the fists tightly. **2** Move to the left into left front stance, left down block. **3** Step forwards into a right front stance, right stepping punch. **4** Move the weight over the back (left) foot, pull the front foot back. Prepare for a right down block. **5** Slide the right foot through and turn into right front stance, a right down block. **6** Step forwards into left front stance, left stepping punch. **7** Pull the front (left) foot and hand back and pivot 90 degrees to the left. Prepare for a left down block. **8** Push the left foot forwards into a front stance, left down block. **9** Step forwards into a right front stance, right stepping punch. **10** Step forwards into a left front stance, left stepping punch. **11** Step forwards into a right front stance, right stepping punch. Shout *'KIAI'*. **12** Pivot on the heel of the right foot and turn the body anti-clockwise. Prepare for a left down block. **13** Turn into a left front stance, left down block.

KARATE

Sparring
(kumite)

Sparring is the practice of karate techniques with a partner. You must control your techniques and emotions to avoid injuring your partner. In sport karate, deliberately hitting an opponent will lead to disqualification. Accidental contact is made in karate, but competitors should not use full force. It requires fast reflexes, good timing and an understanding of the correct distance for each technique.

1 Attacker in basic ready stance, defender ready to block.

2 Attacker moves forward to punch, defender moves back to block.

BLOCK AND COUNTER TO BODY PUNCH

1 Attacker in basic ready stance, defender ready to block.

2 Attacker moves forward to punch, defender moves back to block.

BLOCK AND COUNTER TO HEAD KICK

1 Attacker and defender face each other in a fighting stance.

A strong 'kiai' shows good fighting spirit.

3 Attacker punches to the head, defender performs rising block.

4 Defender counter-attacks with reverse punch to the body.

A basic pre-arranged sparring drill in which the attacker can move forwards with five, three or one step(s). The defender should move back smoothly and block with good timing.

3 Attacker punches to the body, defender performs outside block.

4 Defender counter-attacks with reverse punch to the head.

The fighter on the right moves inside the kick ready to counter-attack with a sweep or throw.

2 Attacker performs a roundhouse kick to the head, defender blocks with both hands.

3 Defender counter-attacks with roundhouse kick to the body.

Self-defence techniques
(goshin jutsu)

The most traditional use of karate techniques is as a way of protection against an attacker. You should only use as much force as necessary to stop an attacker from hurting you.

DEFENCE AGAINST A LAPEL GRAB

Attacker grabs your lapels.

Step back and force his arms apart. Step back to cause the attacker to lose his balance.

Counter-attack by driving the knee of your rear leg into his stomach or groin.

Pull the attacker on to the counter-attack to maximize the effect of the blow. This is a dangerous technique and should only be used when no other choice is available.

DEFENCE AGAINST A HOOK PUNCH

1 **2** **3** **4**

1 Attacker punches at the head with a right hook.
2 Slightly step away from the punch and block with your left forearm. **3** Wrap your left arm around the attacker's arm and apply leverage to the elbow joint. Be careful when you practise this with a partner; only apply minimum force. **4** Counter-attack with a palm heel strike to the chin.

The heel of the hand should strike with enough force to drive the head backwards, stunning the opponent and forcing him off balance.

Useful information

There are many karate styles and associations which promote and teach traditional Karate-do and associated arts. Contact the following for information on the locations of clubs, training methods and styles.

BRITISH KARATE ASSOCIATION
www.britishkarateassociation.co.uk

AUSTRALIAN KARATE FEDERATION
www.akf.com.au/

KAZOKU KAI INTERNATIONAL
www.kazoku.fsnet.co.uk

SHITO-RYU KARATE-DO KOFUKAN
INTERNATIONAL
www.kofukan.com

All the Internet addresses (URLs) given in this book were valid at the time of going to press. However, due to the dynamic nature of the Internet, some addresses may have changed, or sites may have ceased to exist since publication. While the author and publishers regret any inconvenience this may cause readers, no responsibility for any such changes can be accepted by either the author or the publishers.

BRITISH KARATE ASSOCIATION
28 Swan Street,
Manchester,
M4 5JQ

AUSTRALIAN KARATE
FEDERATION
22 Kilolman Street,
The Gap 4061,
Brisbane,
Queensland,
Australia
Tel: 617 3300 0022

KAZOKUKAI KARATE-DO
ASSOCIATION
190 Cannock Road,
Westcroft,
Near Wolverhampton,
Staffordshire,
WV10 8QP
Tel: 01902 865070

SHITO-RYU KARATE-DO KOFUKAN
INTERNATIONAL
Beck House,
Town Street,
Westbrough,
Newark,
Nottinghamshire,
NG23 5HQ

Karate terms

age empi rising elbow strike

age uke rising block

ashi barai foot sweep

choku zuki standing punch

chudan body

dojo martial arts training hall

empi elbow

gedan barai down block, lower
sweeping block

gohon kumite five step sparring

Goju ryu hard and soft (name of
a karate style)

goshin jutsu self-defence
techniques

gyaku zuki reverse punch

hiji elbow

ippon kumite one step sparring

jiyu kumite free style sparring

jodan head

kata form

kiai shout

kiba dachi straddle stance

kihon basic

kizami zuki jab punch

kokutsu dachi back stance

kumite sparring

mae geri front kick

mawashi geri roundhouse kick

neko ashi dachi cat stance

oi zuki basic punch

sanbon kumite three step
sparring

Shito Ryu name of a karate style

Shotokan Shoto's Hall (name of a
karate style)

shuto uke knifehand block

sanchin dachi three battles
stance

soto uke outside block

tachi stances

Taikyoku 'Great Ultimate' – the
older name for *kihon kata*

tsuru ashi dachi crane stance

uchi uke inside block

uraken back fist

ushiro empi rear elbow strike

ushiro geri back kick

Wado Ryu The Way of Peace
(name of a karate style)

yoko empi elbow side strike

yoko geri side kick

yoko geri keage side snap kick

yoko geri kekomi side thrust kick

zenkutsu dachi front stance

Index